IT'S A BOA CONSTRICTOR!

by Tessa Kenan

BUMBA BOOKS™

LERNE

Note to Educators:

Throughout this book, you'll find critical thinking questions. These can be used to engage young readers in thinking critically about the topic and in using the text and photos to do so.

Lerner Publications Company
A division of Lerner Publishing Group, Inc.
241 First Avenue North
Minneapolis, MN 55401 USA

For reading levels and more information, look up this title at www.lernerbooks.com.

Library of Congress Cataloging-in-Publication Data

Names: Kenan, Tessa, author.
Title: It's a boa constrictor! / by Tessa Kenan.
Other titles: It is a boa constrictor!
Description: Minneapolis : Lerner Publications, [2017] | Series: Bumba books. Rain forest animals | Includes bibliographical references and index. | Audience: Age 4–8. | Audience: K to grade 3.
Identifiers: LCCN 2016021989 (print) | LCCN 2016026869 (ebook) | ISBN 9781512425673 (lb : alk. paper) | ISBN 9781512429312 (pb : alk. paper) | ISBN 9781512427578 (eb pdf)
Subjects: LCSH: Boa constrictor—Juvenile literature. | Rain forest animals—Juvenile literature.
Classification: LCC QL666.O63 K45 2017 (print) | LCC QL666.O63 (ebook) | DDC 597.96/7—dc23

LC record available at https://lccn.loc.gov/2016021989

Manufactured in the United States of America
1 – VP – 12/31/16

Expand learning beyond the printed book. Download free, complementary educational resources for this book from our website, www.lerneresource.com.

Table of Contents

Boas Slither

Boa constrictors

are snakes.

They live in rain forests.

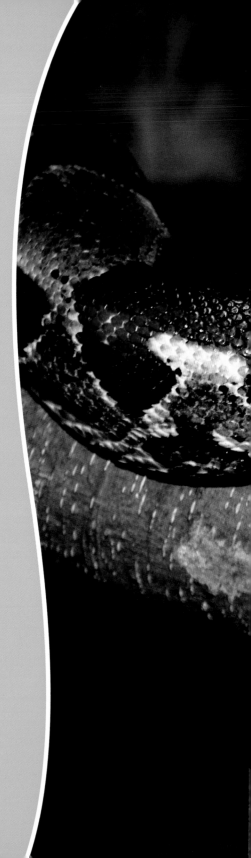

Boas can swim.

But they usually stay on land.

They can live in empty logs.

Sometimes they live in burrows.

Boas can be different colors.

They can have different markings

on their skin too.

This boa is green.

Why do you think boas can be different colors?

Boas hunt at night.

Their jaws open wide.

Boas use small teeth to catch and hold prey.

Why would it be helpful for boas to open their jaws wide?

Then boas constrict

their prey.

They wrap their bodies

tightly around it.

This slowly kills

the prey.

The boa swallows its

prey whole.

Mother boas can have sixty babies at one time.

They leave their mother right away.

Baby boas already know

how to hunt.

They also know how to hide

from larger animals.

What kinds of animals might baby boas hunt?

Boas grow to be very big.

They keep growing as they

get older.

They can be as long as a car!

Boas live alone.

They can live to be thirty

years old.

Parts of a Boa Constrictor

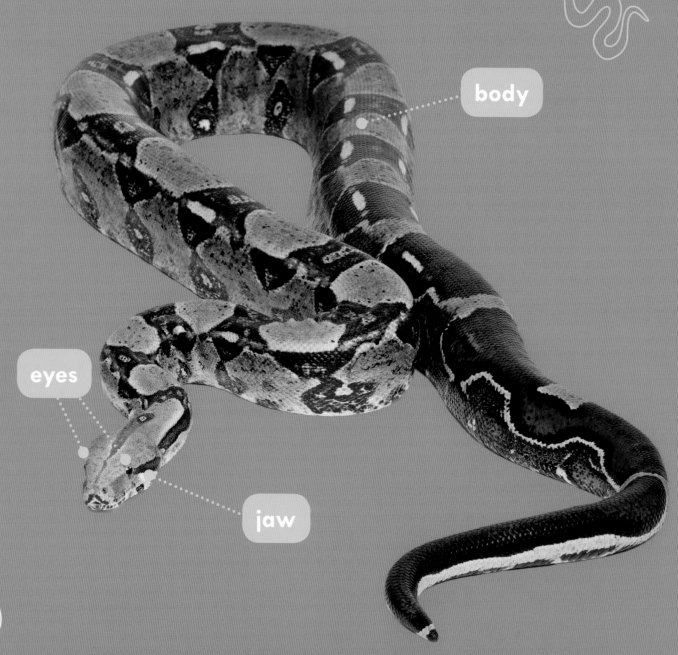

body

eyes

jaw

Picture Glossary

burrows

holes or tunnels animals dig in the ground

constrict

to squeeze

prey

animals that are hunted by other animals

rain forests

thick, tropical forests where lots of rain falls

23

Index

Read More

Hansen, Grace. *Snakes*. Minneapolis: Abdo Kids, 2015.

Rake, Matthew. *Scaly, Slippery Creatures*. Minneapolis: Hungry Tomato, 2016.

Raum, Elizabeth. *Taipans*. Mankato, MN: Amicus High Interest/Amicus Ink, 2016.

Photo Credits